EDWARD A. ARMSTRONG

Discovering
Bird Song

SHIRE PUBLICATIONS LTD.

Contents

ACKNOWLEDGEMENTS

The original sonagrams were kindly made for this book by Mrs Joan Hall-Craggs at the University of Cambridge Sub-department of Animal Behaviour from discs in the BBC archives except for the Blackcap and imitations (fig. 29) recorded by Mr V. C. Lewis (Pye Records Ltd). I gratefully acknowledge her help and the assistance of the sub-department as well as the kindness of the BBC and the recordists in giving permission for their recordings to be used: J. Burton, fig. 20; J. Hall-Craggs, fig. 30 (below); V. C. Lewis, figs. 1 and 29; B. Margoschis, fig. 26; E. Simms, fig. 30 (above); M. Sinclair, fig. 5; O. Unger, fig. 21. Miss M. Vince kindly gave permission for the use of fig. 27.

My thanks are also expressed to the writers and publishers who gave permission for the reproduction of illustrations from their publications. I am also grateful to Mr R. A. Hume for his sketches which enliven the text (figs. 6, 8, 11, 13, 14, 17, 19, 22, 23, 24, 25), and to the photographers listed below.

I am very grateful to Mrs Hall-Craggs and Professor W. H. Thorpe for reading this book in typescript. By easing my responsibilities in various ways my wife, Eunice, has greatly facilitated my work.

                                             EDWARD A. ARMSTRONG
                                                         Cambridge

The cover design by Ron Shaddock shows a Blackbird 'chinking' with a sonagram of the sound as background.

Photographs are acknowledged as follows: Edward A. Armstrong, plates 3, 8, 10; Australian News and Information Bureau, plate 6; Miss Terry Gompertz, plate 14; Richard T. Mills, plates 1, 2, 4, 5, 7, 9, 11, 12; Miss E. L. Turner, plate 15; J. van Peppel, plate 13.

Introduction: enjoying bird song

Among life's pleasures one of the greatest is to listen to birds singing, especially when there is a glorious outburst of song early on a spring morning, whether we hear it comfortably in bed or, as is more trouble but much more thrilling, in the woods before dawn as one species after another joins in the chorus. The abilities of birds as songsters and other aspects of their behaviour — their sprightliness, remarkable displays and expertise in nest-building — excite our interest and admiration. They are the only creatures besides ourselves which we speak of naturally and appropriately as singing.

Bird song—and by that we mean all the utterances of birds—has artistic as well as scientific interest. Birds challenge us to realise that their music is in some respects comparable with our own, in others very different. Some utter sounds which to us are very pleasing, emotionally and musically. Human delight in singing birds is evident throughout the ages in the literatures of many countries. Scientifically, bird song has so many fascinating aspects that in this brief survey only a few can be mentioned. A bird's songs not only have interest, and often beauty, in their own right but should be regarded as patterns of behaviour, linked with many others, which enable the singer to live in harmony with an intricate environment. They are the product of remarkable vocal organs brought into action by subtle physiological changes correlated with alterations in a bird's surroundings, including vocal and visual stimulation from other birds.

Only recently, with the invention of devices for recording and 'picturing' bird song in sonagrams, has it been possible to study its structure scientifically and to discover more clearly what it is all about. It is with this aspect — the way in which birds influence each other by their vocalisations — that we are here most concerned. What is the significance of their songs and calls for the birds themselves? Why should these be so various? How do a bird's utterances ensure its being in appropriate relationship with its fellows? How are they adapted to its environment? We can, indeed, enjoy bird song without asking ourselves such questions but whether it is a matter of watching a football match, admiring a picture or appreciating our friends, understanding adds depth to our pleasure.

The bird-watcher, or, as we might call him, the 'bird-listener', who wishes to discover the interest and significance of bird song, has various aids available, some of which are mentioned at the end of this book. If he finds it difficult to recognise and memorise songs and calls he may make use of the time-honoured device of putting them into words. The Yellowhammer sings *a little bit of bread and no cheese*, the Great Tit calls *teacher, teacher*; the

3

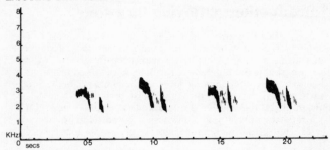

1. Sonagram of a fragment of Song Thrush song illustrating reiteration. The horizontal scale shows the duration of the sound, the vertical scale its frequency; the higher the trace the higher the sound. A trace extending almost from top to bottom is without definite pitch — a 'noise' — while a substantial mark at a point on the vertical plane indicates a sound which we would adjudge musical.

Chiffchaff, Cuckoo, Kittiwake and Curlew announce their names, and the Corn Bunting's song resembles the jingling of a bunch of keys. The poets have tried to help us — with varying success. Shakespeare's Skylark chants *tirra lirra* and Lyly's Nightingale cries *jug, jug, jug, tereu*. Browning noticed 'the wise Thrush, he sings each song twice over' (fig. 1).

Illustrated handbooks give brief details of the vocalisations of each species and many recordings are available on discs and tape. One's own notebook becomes increasingly valuable as interest and experience increase. To list all the different utterances of any one species of bird and the occasions on which they are heard requires time and patience but is a worthwhile achievement.

There is no better short cut to discovering bird song than to roam around with a knowledgeable friend. Membership of a bird club or natural history society paves the way to such friendships. The best time to start is in early spring. While the trees are leafless identification is easier, you can notice how song develops, and more species are heard as the season advances. Having learned the songs of the common resident species you are better able to identify the migrants as they arrive and announce their presence in song. Outings and holidays provide opportunities for becoming acquainted with species further afield. Camping is an ideal way of getting among birds in out of the way places and acquiring the feeling of being a little like a bird oneself.

Even in a district of suburban gardens there are usually ten or more different song-birds to be heard in spring. As I write in a Cambridge garden there are around: Blackbird, Song Thrush,

Robin, Wren, Starling, Hedgesparrow, Great Tit, Blue Tit, Greenfinch, Goldfinch, Chaffinch and Collared Dove. Those of us who live in any part of the British Isles have the advantage of being able to reach various kinds of habitat — river, marsh, woodland, mountain and sea-coast — with comparative ease and thus become acquainted with the songs and calls of many different species. The diversity of birds in a tropical forest is greater than in temperate-zone woodlands, and yet it would be difficult, perhaps impossible, to stand anywhere in such a forest and hear as many good singers as can be heard in our springtime woods and gardens.

As our interest, attention and understanding increase we become more sensitive to what we hear and better able to distinguish niceties which earlier we had not noticed. We discover that the birds are speaking to us in a language we can understand and so we become participants in their world. Our sympathies expand, our enjoyment increases and our lives are enriched.

1. Bird language

The sounds which birds utter are their way of talking to one another. Many of these sounds are musical, some are non-vocal or instrumental, but they are, above all, practical. They constitute language; so we shall first discuss the kinds of information they communicate, giving attention to call-notes as well as song proper and remembering that song can include information carried by call-notes but is normally more informative than any single call.

Bird repertoires

Not many birds have more than twenty-five distinctive signal utterances but in this respect birds are better endowed than mammals. Even the noisy and voluble howler monkey and gibbon have vocabularies of about thirteen and between fifteen and twenty calls respectively. We are separated from all other living creatures by an enormous gulf so far as what we can communicate is concerned. The difference is due to human powers of thought, not vocal limitations, for some birds can imitate speech (see Chapter 5). Estimates of the number of distinctive utterances characteristic of various species are approximate as observers use different criteria and only after years of studying a species can an observer feel confident that he knows all its songs and calls, as well as the situations in which they are uttered. The White Stork has three calls, the Jay and Treecreeper six, the Herring Gull eight and the Jackdaw nine. The Robin has three kinds of song, five signal sounds uttered by adults and two by the young. The Chaffinch has thirteen adult call-notes in addition to song. Adult male Great Tits have at least twenty-six distinct calls as well as at least four variations on the *teacher, teacher* song. Probably study of other birds as detailed as has been devoted to these tits would reveal undetected nuances in their calls. The Wren's repertoire consists of about thirteen adult call-notes, three characteristic of the young and four types of song — but 'fighting song', abbreviated and congested, seems to be territorial song modified in one direction whereas courtship subsong which is slower, lower-pitched and, to our ears, sweeter, is modified in the other. It may be shorter or much longer than territorial song. Males leading a party to roost sing snatches which might be termed 'roosting song', but this is mentioned to indicate a difficulty in classifying song into types. We may do so according to function or structure — or both. Song used in different situations is not always structurally different. In addition the female sings a very quiet 'whisper song' when concerned with the young — feeding or leading them (Chapter 4). Only one call of thirteen is reckoned as a fighting call but during close-up encounters several kinds of brief utterance are heard. The Pied Flycatcher is reported to have seventeen types of utterance, including song, and the Chukar Partridge fourteen adult calls.

The calls as well as the songs of birds may be modified so that they acquire changed significance. For example, the vehemence with which an alarm sound is uttered may indicate the degree of danger to be apprehended. Many calls are appropriate only in certain relationships, such as between parent and young (Chapter 4). Some, mostly those associated with breeding, are confined to a particular season. Commonly calls not only convey information but stimulate to action or compel inaction — as when a parent's alarm note causes a chick to 'freeze'. Information and stimulation are closely linked.

Human language and bird language

Human language is adapted to express our thoughts and emotions. When we use the term 'language' in connection with birds we must be on our guard lest we think of them as limited, inferior human beings; but equally it is mistaken to regard them as mechanisms 'triggered' into action by certain sounds. Their language, like that of babies, is limited to the extent that they can express only their feelings and reactions at the moment. The fact that we have to judge the meaning of an utterance by the reaction it evokes in another bird is no justification for thinking of birds as little different from machines — as some specialists seem to do. At the other extreme we need to remember that when poets write of the Skylark 'rejoicing' and the Dove as 'mourning' they are referring to how these bird's utterances make them feel. What these birds feel is another matter — about which we know little. We must not think of birds in a merely sentimental way, nor yet in a mean way. They are lively, vivid, mysterious creatures with behaviour in some respects comparable to our own and in other respects very different. These similarities and differences make them fascinating. In studying birds we need sympathetic insight as well as scientific interest.

Information communicated by bird language

With the reservations suggested we may translate certain bird calls directly into words, such as 'flee' and 'approach', or render some vocalisations into sentences, as for instance: 'any male intruder of my own species will meet with opposition'. It is because many utterances convey more than can be expressed in one word that we speak of bird 'repertoires' rather than 'vocabularies'. We may list some of the information communicated thus:
Identity (species; sex; individuality; status); *Motivation* (agonistic;

2. *Simplified sonagrams illustrating the classes of auditory signal of the Domestic Fowl. (N. E. Collias in 'Animal Sounds and Communication', ed. W. E. Lanyon and W. N. Tavolga, Amer. Inst. Biol. Sci., 1960.)*

Structure		Signal
HIGH-PITCHED, HARSH		
continuous		aerial predator
segmented		ground predator
LOW-PITCHED		
long, harsh notes		threat
brief, soft notes		clucking
HARMONIC		
continuous		crowing
segmented		food
CHANGING PITCH		
up		pleasure
down		distress

alarm; appetitive; distress or well-being); *Environmental*
(location of and reaction to: individuals; objects; territory;
predators).

IDENTITY

Specific identity

The sounds made by different species are so distinctive that an
experienced ornithologist could be led blindfold through a wood in
spring and be able to name all the birds singing. He might be
puzzled by some calls because some contact and other notes of
various species are rather similar. Birds are able to distinguish
details in the utterances of their own kind better than we can. A
Garden Warbler in good voice can be mistaken for a mediocre
Blackcap but the birds themselves are not deceived. By detailed
analysis of a song we are able to discover that certain of its
characteristics give one kind of information, while other features
have a different function. However, most call-notes are distinctive
to our ears and even more so to the birds. The Chaffinch's *pink*,
the Goldfinch's soft *switt-witt-witt-witt* and the Bullfinch's quiet,
piping contact call reveal unmistakably the identity of the birds;

3a. Sonagram of the drumming of the Lesser Spotted Woodpecker.

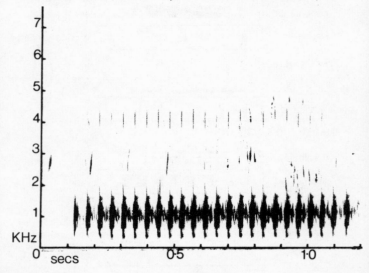

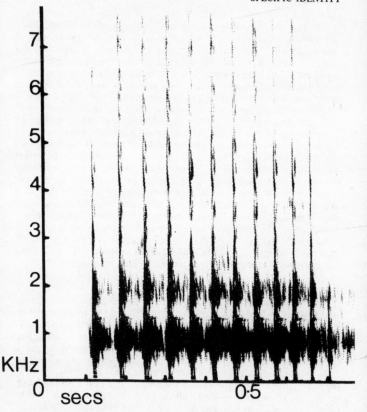

3b. Sonagram of the drumming of the Great Spotted Woodpecker.

so with the caw of the Rook, the snarl of the Carrion Crow, the harsh chatter of the Magpie and the Jay's raucous scream. Thus the calls of birds belonging to the same family declare their identity to us and even more distinctively to members of their own species. Song, being more complex, is particularly effective in revealing identity. A bird may deceive another by imitating its call but this is rare and usually accidental. Even when communication is by the simple procedure of tapping on a branch the calls are distinctive. No species of woodpecker in any given area 'drums' exactly like any other (fig. 3).

Sex

During the breeding season it is essential that birds should unambiguously make known their sex. At close range this is achieved by forms of visual display. In many species sex identification is aided by differences in plumage and other adornments but the sense of smell, so important among mammals, is not used. Stimulatory calls and songs may also be effective in courtship, but for long-range sex identification territorial song is important. Normally it is a declaration of masculinity. Exceptional hen birds may sing, mainly due to endocrine imbalance, as when a superannuated female Blackbird utters crude snatches of song or an elderly Domestic Fowl tries to crow. However, in some species females defend territory with song and there are many in which the female utters non-territorial song. A male bird normally replies to territorial song, so in species in which the sexes look alike a silent bird in a male's territory is liable to be treated as a female. A mated cock Robin will tolerate another non-singing Robin in his territory. I have known such a bird, presumably a female, feed the chicks for a day when the mated female gave up exhausted after the cock had failed to assist. When I placed a mounted Wren in a male's domain he approached and sang excitedly but as there was no reply he tried to copulate with it.

Individuality

When birds are closely associated they become able to recognise one another individually. To some extent they do so by appearance but vocalisations commonly play an important part. A semi-somnolent Hawfinch immediately flies off the nest on hearing her mate's call even though other Hawfinches are calling. Many gulls may be screaming overhead but a Herring Gull, dozing on her eggs, awakens and looks up when her mate calls. Similarly, despite the clamour of its neighbours, a Gannet at the nest in a crowded colony recognises the mate's call as he or she flies in to alight. Chicks of the Common and Sandwich Tern respond only to the parental call (fig. 4) — 'Here comes Mum (or Dad) with a fish'. Antarctic explorers, noticing that young penguins massed together in 'crèches', thought that when an adult arrived with food it was a case of 'first come, first served' but it is now known that the chicks recognise and respond to the calls of their parents.

Guillemots, which in their behaviour have much in common with penguins, breed in colonies, one of which in Norway has been estimated to consist of almost 100,000 pairs. The single egg is laid without nest material on a cliff ledge or a flat-topped rock-stack where the birds are so crowded that it is almost 'standing-room only'. The chorus of calling is terrific. If a parent is disturbed and flies away the chick tries to hide in a crevice but when she returns and gives the appropriate call it responds immediately and comes

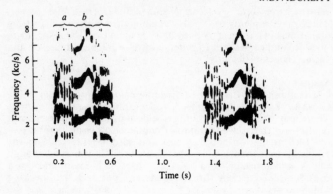

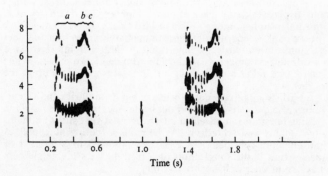

4. Two consecutive calls of individual Sandwich Terns. Each call is divided into three segments. It is apparent that the calls of the two birds differ. (M. E. Hutchinson, J. Stevenson, and W. H. Thorpe, 'Behaviour' 32, 1968.)

to be brooded. If a recording is now played the chick leaves its warm sconce amidst its parent's feathers and goes to the loudspeaker. Earlier in its life, even in the egg, it utters calls to which the parents reply. Thus parents and chick get to know each other individually (Chapter 4).

Jackdaws in a flock identify each other as individuals and if one returns after some weeks away they still recognise him or her. There may be plenty of Jackdaws calling near where one is sitting on her nest in a tree cavity but when her mate calls she responds to his voice and comes out. In general, birds order their domestic and social affairs efficiently.

Status

The absence of disorder in breeding colonies and flocks is due to birds 'knowing their place', topographically and in society. There may be squabbling but it is seldom disruptive. In a hen run poultry sort themselves out into a dominance order or hierarchy — one bird at the top becomes boss and so down the scale to the miserable individual who is subordinate to all the others. Although this is sometimes called a 'pecking order' it is maintained to a considerable extent by threat sounds and postures. The pecking which occurs is aggravated by the cramped conditions in which the birds are confined. Normally among higher animals threat sounds and displays take the place of blows. Fights to the death are most unusual, whether among wolves or bird flocks. In a Jackdaw flock the boss only keeps in order those immediately below him and does not bully other birds. A high-ranking bird will interfere in a chivalrous way on behalf of the subordinate of two others. When such a bird takes a mate she gains his status and 'goes up in the world'.

A bird's song reveals not only its sex but its maturity and vigour. It may also indicate whether or not he has secured a mate. A Wren seeking to establish himself in a territory is at first silent and later sings quietly and tentatively. As he gains a footing he expresses himself more confidently. It has been observed in a number of species that if the songfulness of a bird declines his neighbours may try to encroach on his territory.

MOTIVATION

Agonistic

This term has come into use because it includes offensive and defensive activities. Territorial song, as is already evident, involves an agonistic or pugnacious component, but threat or warning calls are important in any bird's repertoire of utterances. The seriousness of a threat is often indicated by the loudness, harshness and reiteration of the call as well as by the individual's posture, but menacing sounds vary according to species and circumstances. A Domestic Cock makes a low grumbling noise as a warning to other fowl (2) but some birds utter loud screams or threat songs.

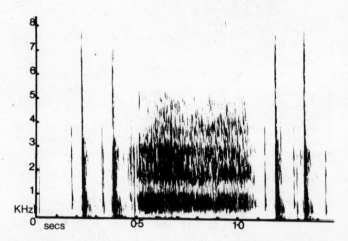

5. *Defensive utterances of Snowy Owl chick. The vertical traces record bill-snapping, the confused markings represent hissing.*

Hissing is a common threat sound, characteristic of birds as different as the Ostrich, Kiwi, Mute Swan (plate 3), Snowy Owl (figs. 5 and 6) and various song birds. When a Greylag Goose advances with outstretched neck cackling gently he is making a friendly gesture but if he hisses a threat is intended. The cock American Ruffed Grouse erects his ruff and tail, menacing a rival with hisses, and a Yellow Wagtail hisses at another male. White Storks, young and old, which are among the least vocal of birds, express annoyance by hissing. Some hole-nesting birds, such as the Hoopoe, hiss when within the cavity to deter intruders. Probably the similarity of the sound to that made by snakes adds to its

13

6. Snowy Owl.

effectiveness. A Wryneck, brooding in a woodpecker's disused nest-hole, hisses when disturbed and the protests made by nestling woodpeckers of some species sound like hissing. Nestlings of the Hairy Woodpecker, an American species, buzz like swarming bees when disturbed — possibly a protective adaptation, as bees often hive in tree cavities just as, in North America, snakes occasionally take refuge in woodpecker holes.

The behaviour of the tits, Great and Blue, is of special interest in this connection. When I placed my finger in a hole where a Blue Tit was nesting I was startled by a loud, explosive hissing sound. I discovered that it was due to the sitting bird's wings being suddenly flipped out and back, brushing against the sides of the

7. Blackbird alarm calls: (a) tchook; (b) hoarse musical outcry; (c) chink; (d) thin call, warning of raptor overhead, but used on other occasions when startled. (G. Thielcke, 'Vogelstimmen', Springer Verlag, 1970.)

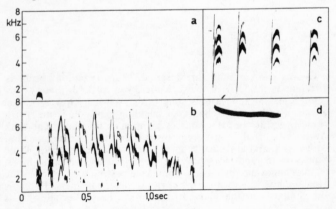

cavity. The bird repeated these movements and swishing sounds again and again every time I darkened the entrance. The sounds closely resemble those a snake might make, shuffling and hissing. Some other tits, including the Great Tit, behave similarly (plate 14). Undoubtedly a squirrel, weasel or stoat would be intimidated. We may assume that the ancestors of our tits acquired this behaviour in Asia where snakes are a more serious menace to nesting birds than in colder regions. Another remarkable adaptation to deter predators is the likeness of the young Burrowing Owl's call when cornered in the burrow to the prairie rattlesnake's rattle — due to selection rather than imitation.

Alarm

When a bird is startled and flies away it may emit a call, much as you or I might cry 'oh!' On hearing a shout we look around to find out what is the matter. So do birds when they hear certain sounds. Thus alarm calls serve as alerting or warning signals to neighbouring birds of the same, or sometimes other, species. They differ according to circumstances and the species involved. Many have more than one such call, used according to the degree of alarm or the nature of the marauder. The Blackbird has five such calls, three indicating minor or major anxiety, one denoting a flying predator, and a scream when the bird is seized (fig. 7). The

8. Oxpeckers.

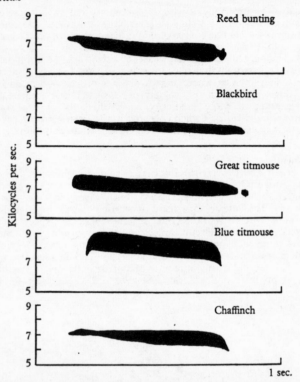

9. Calls of five different species when a hawk flies over. They all sound like a high thin whistle. (P. Marler, in 'Darwin's Biological Work', ed. P. R. Bell, C.U.P., 1959.)

reactions of neighbouring birds vary. Birds are innately equipped to utter certain warning sounds and also to respond to them when heard. They also learn to take warning from the alarm movements and calls of other species. When the Oxpeckers (fig. 8) busy searching for ticks on a giraffe's neck or the back of a rhinoceros suddenly take flight the animal looks around to see what has disturbed them. Similarly, the gamekeeper suspects that poachers are in the coverts when he hears an outcry from the Pheasants. The extent to which alarm reactions are instinctive or learned varies according to the species and depends a good deal on how social it is. Jackdaws spontaneously give the alarm call and make a mass attack on seeing something black and dangling, even a black feather carried by one of their number bearing a very remote resemblance to a Jackdaw seized by a predator. All else is a matter of learning what is dangerous.

As prompt reaction to a danger signal may make all the difference between life and death, different species often respond to each others' signals just as ships at sea, whatever their nationality, immediately recognise and respond to the 'mayday' distress signal. The calls uttered by a number of species of small bird when a hawk or falcon flies over are so similar that they constitute a general warning — a thin, high whistle (fig. 9). This *seeet* note is difficult to locate and therefore does not betray the position of the caller, whereas the calls uttered by birds mobbing an owl are easily located and attract different species to join in slanging it (fig. 10). They proclaim 'danger is lurking here'. Where two species are closely associated they learn to respond to each other's alarm calls and actions. The Pygmy Owl preys diurnally on small birds. If its whistling call is imitated Coal Tits and

10. Calls of seven different species when mobbing an owl. (P. Marler, in 'Darwin's Biological Work', ed. P. R. Bell, C.U.P., 1959.)

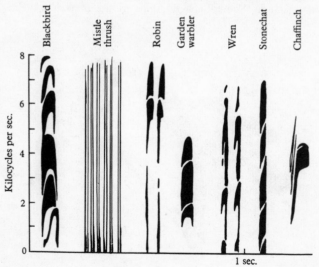

Treecreepers are attracted. This is adaptive because if the lurking-place of a predator is known it cannot so easily carry out surprise attacks.

Birds which have seen one of their number attacked may become hypersensitive and react mistakenly. The Oropendola is a large dark bird with a scanty crest and very conspicuous yellow tail feathers. I spent some time in the Central American forest within view of a huge tree festooned with their nests — woven pouches suspended from the tips of branches out of reach of the howler monkeys. The females are exposed to birds of prey as they cling to their nests while building, so the males act as sentinels and sound a loud *cack-cack-cack* when a raptor appears. Then they all dive into the foliage. But sometimes they become careless and react slowly. They go to the other extreme when a hawk seizes a building bird. For some time afterwards there are frequent false alarms.

Appetitive

Motivation of this kind is involved when a bird seeks the satisfaction of some need or drive, particularly the basic drives of hunger and sex. Nestlings make their hearty appetites known by a cheeping chorus — though its intensity and frequency is related to the extent to which the chicks are vulnerable to marauders. Buntings utter two kinds of begging call — close-up and long-range. The long-range call develops only when the young are about to leave the nest. It is such that the parents may locate their chicks in vegetation. Young Snow Buntings are exceptional as they call

11. Great Tits.

loudly and frequently while in the nest but when they leave it their calls are intermittent and muted. These adaptations are easily explained; the chicks are safe from the Arctic fox in a crevice deep underneath a rock but they are very vulnerable on the tundra.

The vigour with which nestlings plead tends to regulate the amount of food they get. Noisy sit-ins produce results. When six of a brood of seven nestling Pied Flycatchers were removed the parents soon decreased the supplies they were bringing, but after the six had been replaced out of sight close to the nest and their calling could be heard the parents increased the rate of their feeding visits — with the result that they had to eat the food themselves as the one youngster was soon satiated. The begging calls of nestlings may attract other species to provide them with food. I have seen a Robin feeding young Song Thrushes, a Chaffinch has been known to feed young Hawfinches and sometimes a young Cuckoo's calls induce a bird other than the foster-parents to feed it.

In some species there is a link between the satisfaction of the two urges for food and sex. The Laughing Gull normally feeds the female before copulation and just prior to being mounted a Rook begs for food with the avid movements of a young bird. The female Great Tit's (fig. 11) pleading for the male to 'courtship-feed' her is very similar to the pre-copulatory display. She crouches, uttering a high-pitched call and quivering her wings. Her calls before and during this courtship feeding have points of similarity with the calls of an almost fledged bird (fig. 12). Indeed the behaviour of female birds during courtship feeding appears to be a reversion to the behaviour of a young bird. (When such feeding behaviour occurs between mated birds it may be called 'connubial feeding'). A female Great Tit may pursue her mate, begging, throughout the whole period during which the young are in the nest. Male Marsh and Coal Tits sometimes feed the female after copulation. Common Terns join in noisy fights, the male carrying a fish. When they alight he may present it to the female before treading her.

Sex invitation

The significance of territorial song as a long-distance invitation to pair up is stressed later (Chapter 3) but, when the male has attracted a female and the two birds are close together, visual stimuli, particularly the male's posturing and displays, usually become more important than his utterances — though in many species his calls or songs may excite her sexually. The male usually 'makes the going' but either sex of Great Tit may invite copulation, giving a high-pitched *zeedle-zeedle-zeedle-zee*, and the

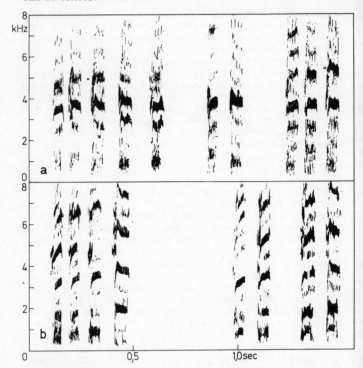

12. Begging calls of (a) Great Tit fledgling, (b) mated female Great Tit. (G. Thielcke, 'Vogelstimmen', Springer Verlag, 1970.)

female Wren may solicit the male, squatting low with quivering wings and emitting a squeal. Among Herring Gulls the female usually takes the initiative in pair-formation, walking round the male with her neck drawn in and occasionally giving a melodious *kleeoo* as she tosses her head. Coition follows after a lengthy ritual. The female goes through the head-tossing procedure, uttering the food-begging call, and the male acts similarly. After a hoarse cry he mounts, continuing this call as he copulates.

Pre-copulatory songs and calls are usually subdued because of the nearness to one another of the pair and their vulnerability. The Greater Honeyguide is exceptional. He perches on a favourite tree and reiterates his loud *whit-purr* and *vic-tor* calls every minute or so for about eight hours day after day. When a female is attracted he copulates with her. There is no further association, unless the female chooses to return, and the 'stud post' has no territorial significance. The 'lek' display of the Blackcock and a number of other species which call at a display arena or isolated stance approximates to this pattern of behaviour.

The nature of the pair-bond, the means by which it is established and the foraging habits of the species are closely related. It might seem that species in which the care of the young devolves entirely on one sex must be handicapped in raising sufficient young to carry on the species, but this is not so. The female Red-necked Phalarope lives free of domestic cares when she has laid the eggs. Male and female Greater Honeyguide both evade responsibility for the family as the species is parasitic. She drops her eggs into other birds' nests as the Cuckoo does. Such differences in behaviour can only be understood when we know more concerning the intricate way in which a bird is adapted to its environment. Brood parasitism should not be thought of merely as one bird taking advantage of another.

Distress or deprivation

Distress calls may be evoked by imminent danger or actual disaster, as when a bird is seized by a predator. Their intensity varies according to the degree of disquiet, danger or pain. It is difficult to draw a clear distinction between alarm and distress calls though in some species the cries of a seized bird are heard at no other time. A Starling screams loudly when carried off by a Sparrowhawk and many birds when taken in the hand shriek or squeal. Such calls may have value as signals, especially among social birds, for others may be attracted and succeed in distracting the predator by their movements, cries and, sometimes, attacks. The screams of a Jackdaw in pain bring others of the flock to mob their comrade's assailant. Although Arctic Terns are small and dainty they dive at and strike an intruder, human or four-footed. I have had to cover my head to protect it from these birds and have seen them drive away a sheep. Birds normally timid may show great persistence in approaching, shrieking at and sometimes attacking the marauder when a chick utters a distress cry.

Deprivation calls are familiar to all who have heard the cheeping of a duckling left behind when the brood was being led to the water. To our ears they sound plaintive and pleading. They are also effective as location signals, informing the parent where to find the chick. They tend to be inflected downwards in pitch;

contentment calls are inflected upwards (fig. 2). To us these seem expressive of well-being. Contentment calls, such as we hear when chicks nestle under their mother's breast, are in strong contrast with distress calls which are loud and harsh, as with man and other mammals. This similarity of response to certain extreme types of utterance is of interest as 'one touch of nature' which 'makes the whole world kin'.

Deprivation calls of another type are those uttered by a member of a mated pair when the partner is out of sight.

ENVIRONMENT

Location of individuals and contact calls

Many of the call-notes already considered also rank as contact calls in so far as they indicate where the caller is located. Others, particularly the calls of newly fledged nestlings and 'flying predator' warnings, give few localisation clues (fig. 9). Many species have contact calls other than those used in the parent-chick or male-female relationships. Often our first intimation that a party of Long-tailed Tits is around is hearing their conversation consisting of various calls — *tupp tsirrup* and a high-pitched *zee-zee-zee*. Here and there the dainty gymnasts dart from twig to twig searching for minute insects. Soon they have disappeared — for the flock drifts away through the bushes seeking fresh hunting-grounds. Sometimes Goldcrests, Coal Tits or Marsh Tits join the party. Long-tailed Tits are exceptionally social to the extent that a third bird may aid a pair in feeding the nestlings. In winter roosting parties huddle together to keep warm. It is obviously to the advantage of Long-tailed Tits to maintain contact. The mixed groups which move through tropical forests probably profit through the general disturbance making varied prey available. Individuals of the 'leader' species flush insects which are seized by other species in the flock. Since no two have the same food preferences the different species are not as much in competition as they might seem to be.

Chevrons of geese flying by night on migration or moving from one feeding area to another keep up a constant gaggling which enables them to keep in formation and avoid collisions in darkness or going through clouds or fog. The wing music of the Mute Swan is effective as a contact call in the same way as the resonant vocal flight call of the Whooper — named from its call. Among the most thrilling experiences a naturalist can enjoy is the chorus of honking and bugling from wintry waters where hundreds of Bewick's and Whooper Swans are assembling. But most ornithologists who have seen and heard the massed hundreds of thousands of Lesser Flamingoes feeding on an East African lake would agree that so far as numbers, colour and sound are concerned the scene must be described in superlatives.

Location calls enable a bird seeking companions to find them. When a Curlew flies over at night it will respond to a whistled imitation of its cry, waver in flight and temporarily change course (plate 4). Its call is an announcement and an enquiry: 'Here am I. Any other Curlews down there?' Species which 'jug' or roost in a group, such as Partridges and Francolin, utter rallying calls at dusk. If a marauder approaches the probability is that at least one bird will be sufficiently alert to give the alarm.

Location of objects

Besides calling the attention of others to the location of a predator, birds sometimes use calls or songs to indicate where a nest-site or food source is situated. Apart from 'domestic' situations, as when a clucking hen guides her chicks to food, food-location calls are usually uttered when the supply is plentiful or available in quantity for a brief period. One bird's profit is not then to the detriment of another. This situation occurs when a shoal of fish, such as mackerel, appears and gulls exploit the bounteous supply. In such circumstances they utter a food-indication cry and draw attention further by a winding descent flight. Conspicuous white plumage is particularly effective in signalling of this kind. Predominantly white plumage is rare among land birds as it could attract the attention of birds of prey but it is characteristic of many marine species which are vulnerable to the attacks of fewer predators. Its positive value is social, enabling them to make the most of sporadically abundant prey.

Honeyguides get their name from their behaviour in leading men and four-footed mammals to bees' nests. A Stone Age painting of a man robbing bees shows that long ago honey was sought, and we may assume men learned that by following a calling Honeyguide they would gain a luscious reward. Perhaps this guiding behaviour originated when the birds were attracted to where a honeybadger was digging out a nest and in course of time the chattering Honeyguide, associating the honeybadger with a meal, became the leader. It came to regard the animal, and then man, as an ally. We need go no further than our gardens to find an illustration of one component of this chain. A Robin soon appears — and often sings a little — when anyone starts to dig because it associates disturbance of the soil with food. This association was not originally with man. Long before *Homo sapiens* appeared the Robin found it profitable to perch near woodland animals, particularly the wild boar, and forage where the ground and vegetation were being disturbed — just as, in East Africa, Cattle Egrets feed around elephants. When man learned to use a digging stick or other implement the bird was attracted to him. The

Robin's behaviour is inherited, not learned, as is evident when a youngster with speckled breast approaches the gardener.

Among the remarkable aspects of the Honeyguide's behaviour is that after uttering churring notes ahead of a man or animal for a distance in some instances of 200 yards or more the bird does not redouble its outcry near the bees' nest. Its silence indicates that the anticipated plunder is close at hand. As the Honeyguide eats wax, which is not relished by honeybadger or man, guide and guided both profit. Commensalism, in which an organism profits from the feeding behaviour of another species, is widespread throughout the animal kingdom. Fish find shelter beneath the stinging rays of a jellyfish and eat scraps from its meals. Hyenas and jackals know where to go for a feast when they see vultures descending on a carcass.

Location of predators

As we have noted and most people have observed, birds utter alarm cries when they discover a lurking predator or see one approaching. A Blackbird gives a *tchook* note or makes a screaming outcry (fig. 7) and a Wren reiterates chittering calls near where a cat is prowling or lying. Avocets have a specific warning cry uttered when menacing gulls approach the nesting colony. Mammals, too, make sounds which signal the presence of some dangerous creature. In the West African forest squirrels utter a call when they discover a large snake. The natives recognise the significance of this call and follow it up to kill the snake.

Location of territory

By singing a bird indicates the whereabouts of his territory and its extent may be judged by the boundaries where rival males sing against one another.

---

2. Territorial song

Many different kinds of animal from cockroaches to eagles space themselves out by staking a claim to an area and defending it as 'territory'. Territory, as understood by naturalists, has been roughly defined as 'any defended area'. This could be interpreted as including a space no larger than that occupied by a nesting site in a crowded colony of sea-birds — for example, the beak-range of a nesting Gannet — but in practice the term is usually applied to a larger area, some or all of which is used for foraging. Defence may be by the male, the female, the pair or, rarely, a group, and the period involved may be brief or throughout the year. Normally, but not always, the territory is the bird's breeding area and it is defended by song. Usually when bird song is mentioned the reference is to territorial song — the sounds by which a bird gives long-distance notice to all whom it may concern that the area he occupies is private. Those concerned are normally male individuals of the singer's own species. Confusion and fighting are thus avoided, the space necessary for rearing the young is preserved and they can be given the requisite attention. A robust territory owner is seldom evicted although encroaching neighbours may reduce the area originally occupied. He sings vigorously against such birds.

Territorial song is the most informative, most complex and most sustained of a bird's repertoire of utterances. Such song being essential to ensure breeding success and therefore possessing crucial survival value for a species it is not surprising that it is elaborate and distinctive. Expressed in everyday terms a bird singing on a bright May morning is saying loudly to other birds of its kind: 'Here am I, a cock bird, of such-and-such species, an identifiable individual, in my territory, warning off males of my own species, and seeking to attract a mate.'

Not all songs carry this information. In particular a bird may continue singing after he has paired up and is no longer inviting a female to join him, but songfulness may be reduced and even cease for a time. The respites from singing vary according to species, the phases of the breeding cycle and environmental circumstances. To generalise about them is precarious. An unmated female hearing the song of the male of her own species amidst all the other sounds on a spring morning is like a girl awaiting a letter from her boy friend who pays no attention to all the other letters in the morning mail when she notices one addressed in his handwriting. When she reads the letter she may be stimulated to action — to reply accepting the expected invitation to meet. So, too, although emphasis has been placed on the information conveyed by a bird's song, we must also give due importance to its stimulatory effect.

Territorial or advertising song conveys a package of information including some of the items mentioned in the previous chapter in connection with calls. It is: loud, localised, persistent, distinctive, complex and structured.

Loudness

The volume of the territorial song of any species distinguishes it from its other kinds of song, especially courtship song. To be effective it must be heard beyond the boundaries of the territory. A Reed Warbler's song — a rather conversational chattering — can be heard at a distance of 300 yards although the bird's territory is of about 300 square yards, but a Bittern's 'boom' is audible three miles away in good conditions. In contrast, passerines which nest in close proximity to one another, such as Swallows, House and Sand Martins, Lesser Redpolls and some weaverbirds sing in a subdued way. It has been proved experimentally with recordings of birds of the thrush family that quiet songs have reduced effectiveness in deterring intruders. The subdued subsongs of many species, usually sung low down in cover, are not territorial and do not warn off other birds. Of course, loudness is a relative term and must be considered in relation to a bird's size, its habitat and the character of its song.

Localisation

Territorial song gives directional clues, being repetitive, complex and containing features aiding detection of their source. Also, many species make themselves conspicuous visually by flying up while singing, thus increasing the range of the song. Such double conspicuousness must have value great enough to outweigh the increased jeopardy from raptors.

Commonly when a bird has intrusive neighbours he goes near the periphery of his territory to sing, and thus gives notice of its boundaries. Tape recordings of a bird's song may be used to discover the limits of the territory. Even crude imitations may evoke response; whistling will sometimes call forth song from a Nightingale, and a Corncrake can be deceived by drawing a stick over a piece of notched wood, mimicking his rasping double call. The greater the pressure on a bird's domain the more likely he is to protest vehemently by singing loudly close to the intruder. Birds are aware that by singing they challenge other males and so, when they trespass, they do so silently and in a timid or surreptitious way.

A bird may have favourite 'song-stances' in his territory and some species, such as the Tree Pipit (fig. 13), will not settle where

13. Tree Pipit.

suitable points of vantage of this kind are absent. 'Song-stance' or
'call-stance' is preferable to the usual term 'song-post' as the spot
chosen may be on the ground or in low vegetation — reeds or
heather. The Red Grouse springs up from a rock or stone wall,
crowing, and then descends with noisily flapping wings. Later in
the season the birds tend to bring their call-stances closer together
— an approximation to a social display. Blackcock (fig. 14) have
gone further in making their display social for at the 'lek' each
bird has his own call-stance or miniature territory where he
displays, calls and awaits a female. The 'territories' are useless for
foraging. They have become minimal and concentrated together.
Individuals display at and spar with one another and females
come to choose their sex-partners, but lek birds do not pair up
normally, nor does the male assist with rearing the young. This
type of social display with a number of males congregating to show
off and call against one another is characteristic of forest-dwelling
as well as open-ground species — the Cock of the Rock and
manakins of tropical America, some Birds of Paradise, and, in
modified form, the Argus Pheasant and Peacock. The Lyre Bird
displays and sings his song, including mimicries, at more than one
stance in his territory (plate 6). The competitive displays and
calling of lek birds have a stimulating effect on the participants.
Only the Ruff is silent on the display ground. Presumably this
relatively small ground-displaying lek species would not have
survived if, in the open areas it favours, in addition to the
conspicuous and bulky adornments which give the birds their

14. Blackcock.

name, they had added to their vulnerability by calling loudly as many other lek birds do.

Persistence

When a bird is in full song his singing may persist throughout most of the day and even into the night. An observer who timed a Nightingale found that he took only one and a half hours respite during twenty-four hours. A Chaffinch sang 3,300 songs, each of about 2½ seconds duration, in twelve hours, but the record is held by the North American Red-eyed Vireo with 22,197 songs during a day. Many bird activities, including song, are at a maximum in the early morning with another, but lower, peak in the evening. Where there is constant daylight, as in summer in Lapland, some birds, such as the Redwing, may be heard at almost any hour of the day or night, though there is a lull in bird song during the small hours.

The amount of song during the year depends on many factors, including whether the bird is migratory or not, the nature of the pair-bond, the number of broods, and the duration of the moult. The Robin and the Wren, being strongly territorial, may be heard to some extent almost throughout the year. The song Thrush sings during much of the year (fig. 15) but the Mistle Thrush's singing (plate 11) is mainly from January to May.

Reiteration ensures that neighbours are kept informed that a territory is defended. It can be important not only in enabling a bird to obtain a mate but in ensuring that she remains with him. Reed Warblers are liable to lose their mates to bachelor intruders if their singing is insufficiently vigorous. A few birds' songs are very monotonous. In Trinidad a tyrantbird, the Kiskadee, enquired with exasperating regularity for hours on end outside my window in French: 'Qu'est ce qu'il dit?'—'What is he saying?' But close attention to songs such as those of the Chaffinch and some buntings shows that they are not as repetitive as the casual observer might think. These birds have a repertoire of 'song-types' and, after a spell of singing one song-type, change to another. Without recording apparatus these differences are difficult to detect. Some species, including the Chaffinch, utter a call-note which, at short distances, has much of the effectiveness of territorial song in deterring intruders. The Nutcracker maintains territory all the year round with harsh calls. In support of the view that birds have aesthetic sensitivity it has been claimed that in some species the elaboration of territorial song goes beyond biological necessity. This remains a matter on which opinions differ but we may be thankful that songs can be so intricate, pleasing and various, for 'variety is the spice of life'.

Complexity and structure

Even when we listen attentively to songs such as those of the

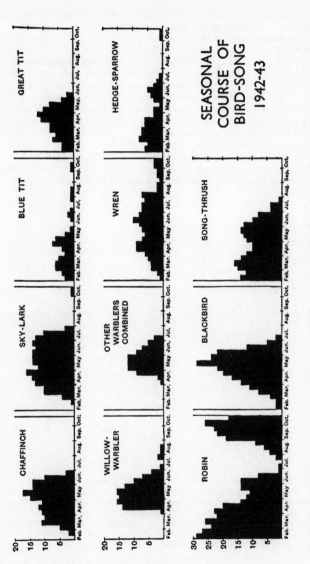

15. Histograms showing the variations in the numbers of individuals of eleven species singing during morning and evening transects from February to October. (P. R. Cox, 'British Birds', 38, 1944.)

Chaffinch and the Wren — comparatively simple phrase songs — we get the impression that more is happening than we can readily take in. Apart from other considerations the rapidity with which many songs are uttered renders it difficult to distinguish separate notes and pitch changes. Birds' powers of discrimination are certainly much better than our own. Sonagrams and recordings played at slow tempi reveal niceties more apparent to the birds than to us. The Wren's song, lasting about five seconds and uttered about five songs to the minute, contains about fifty-six notes — though there is so much slurring in bird songs that to enumerate notes can be misleading.

Roughly speaking, our familiar song-birds utter separate phrases with appreciable pauses between them or more or less continuous songs made up of distinguishable figures, motifs or sub-phrases strung together. New themes are introduced by re-

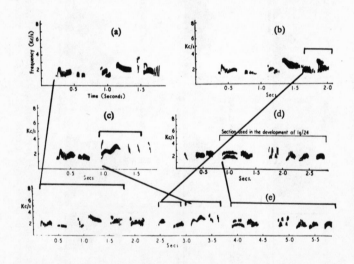

16. The seasonal development of a Blackbird's song. Musical figures extracted from song phrases sung by a Blackbird in the early part of the season (March), and combined to form a long, developed phrase which did not appear in the repertoire until June. (a) phrase 1 (11th March); (b) variant 1a (11th March); (c) variant 1b (11th March); (d) phrase 24 (14th March); (e) developed from 1g/24 (2nd June). (J. Hall-Craggs, 'Ibis' 103, no. 3, 1962.)

combinations of the components (fig. 16). The bunting family represents one type, the thrushes the other.

Distinctiveness

A bird's utterance may be more distinctive than its appearance. Whether you are looking at a Marsh Tit or Willow Tit may be in doubt until you hear the bird's calls. If it calls *pitchew* it is a Marsh Tit. The Chiffchaff and Willow Warbler (plate 2) may be best distinguished by their songs. Two American flycatchers are difficult to tell apart even in the hand but their songs are quite different. As songs are more elaborate than calls they can be, and usually are, more distinctive, revealing even to human ears the bird's species and sometimes its individual identity. They may vary in a number of ways but not beyond the stereotyped limits determined by adaptive requirements. Occasional anomalies occur, as when a Treecreeper learns the song of a Short-toed Treecreeper and so defends his territory from both species.

Songs can be analysed to show that certain components and characteristics are effective in different ways. Thus a tape can be made selecting some components of Robin song which is as effective as the full territorial song in deterring intruders. Some elements may declare a bird's species, others its individual identity.

That a bird's neighbours of his own species recognise his identity by his song is not surprising in view of call-notes being sufficient to reveal identity. The recognitional value of song is apparent when one bird sings against another. In some species,

17. Snipe.

31

and probably in many, a challenged bird replies with the song or song-type in his repertoire most similar to his rival's utterance. This is true of the Chaffinch, Great Tit and Robin. It seems also to be generally true that birds react more strongly to the song of a stranger than to the songs of neighbours. They are able to identify these and, in some circumstances, learn them. This is time and energy saving. The bird registers something like: 'There's old so-and-so in his usual place repeating that song I know so well. I can get on with my own affairs without taking him too seriously.' But if he hears a strange song he knows an intruder is around and must be dealt with.

Instrumental song

Many birds make other than vocal sounds as signals, notably with their wings and bills. These may be equivalent to the vocal songs of other species. The Snipe (fig. 17) protects his territory with a bleating noise created by his wings and outspread tail feathers rushing through the air as he dives high aloft. The Flappet Lark flies over the African grassland and makes with his wings sounds as far-carrying as a Skylark does vocally. The Nightjar claps his wings when a third bird is in his territory. A number of species signal at short range by snapping their mandibles together. Males of some manakins, forest birds of tropical America, make instrumental noises — sharp cracks — with their thickened wing quills as they nimbly jump and flit from twig to twig at the lek. The 'drumming' of woodpeckers, made by rapid blows of the bill on a bough, is their territorial song (fig. 3).

Female song

Territorial song is predominantly a male activity but by no means exclusively so. Female Robins, Starlings, Great Tits and Dippers are among species which sing thus, the first two in autumn. When female Marsh Warblers arrive from winter quarters they may utter brief, feeble songs and occasionally a hen Chaffinch sings imperfectly. There are only a few species in which the roles of the sexes are reversed and the female 'makes the going'. One of these is the dainty Red-necked Phalarope, a northern species nesting sparsely in north-west Ireland and the Hebrides. Females entice the males with a ceremonial flight preceded and followed by special calls. An odd wing-rattling is heard as the birds flit over the marshy ground. When mated, the female attracts her partner to where she is about to lay an egg in a scrape she has prepared in the herbage and on completing the clutch she leaves all responsibilities to him.

Duetting and antiphonal song

In various species the male and female twitter together or utter

1. Sedge Warbler singing among the reeds.

2. Willow Warbler singing.

3. Mute Swan hissing in a defensive posture at Strangford Lough, County Down.

4. Curlew calling in flight.

5. Sparrowhawk calling.

6. Lyrebird singing at its song stance.

7. (Left) Treecreeper calling.

8. (Below) Kittiwake uttering a threat call.

9. Nesting Fulmar Petrels calling.

10. Red-throated Diver approaching its eggs in Shetland.
The call uttered at the nest is a subdued 'ooo'.

11. *Mistle Thrush singing.*

12. *Meadow Pipit singing.*

13. Wren displaying and singing courtship song to his mate.

14. Brooding Great Tit's defensive display. Vocal hissing is combined with a swishing sound made by a sudden downward wing-flip.

15. Nightingale singing subsong to his sitting mate.

antiphonal or reciprocal contact notes. The male's song keeps his mate informed of his whereabouts and may be used to recall her close to him; but there are a number of species, mainly tropical, which sing duets — that is, one bird sings and the other immediately reciprocates so that when the most accomplished of these duettists are concerned it would not be suspected that two birds were involved. Among British birds Little Grebes sing to some extent antiphonally. My first experience of an impressive duet was at dusk on a densely forested island in Central America. Apart from the shrilling of insects all was still when suddenly there rang out loud calls close at hand: *corcorovado, corcorovado.* This emotive, deep fluting continued, getting fainter as the birds ran down to the lake. It is sung by a pair of Marbled Wood Quail, one singing *corcoro,* the other adding *vado.* Thus even at night beneath the dark forest canopy the pair keep in close touch. Only less impressive because uttered in daylight were the duets of three species of bush shrike heard in East Africa. The name of one of them, Boubou Shrike, indicates the resonant, musical repetitive calls (fig. 18) — something between a bell and a toot on a horn. These birds frequent thick foliage and their hootings not only enable contact and mutual rapport to be maintained but also function as territorial songs. The birds vary the pitch of their antiphonal duets in a fascinating way. As many as three or even four individuals may be involved in group performances. Apparently the pair-bond is maintained for life. The significance of duetting in contributing to connubial rapport became apparent when one of a pair died. The survivor began to sing its dead mate's part, as if asking forlornly 'Where are you?'

Fighting song

The pugnacious element in song is most vividly manifested when birds sing during fights. On such comparatively rare occasions the song is distorted, abbreviated, congested or of unusual pitch. Dippers sing incoherently when fighting. Two were seen in a shallow pool striking each other with wings and beaks; one seized and ducked his adversary repeatedly but the bullied bird burst into song each time he got his head above water. When a Wren downed his opponent he sang standing on his body.

Incongruous song

Sometimes excited birds sing in inappropriate situations. When I accidentally frightened young Song Thrushes from the nest the male parent sang a frenzied song perched on the ground. Pied Flycatchers may sing when a bird of prey flies over. When I was at a Skylark's nest the cock gave his flight-song repeatedly close to me. After escaping from a Sparrowhawk, a Skylark will sing and, after being ringed, a Wren flies away singing. These may be

18. Antiphonal songs of the Boubou Shrike from various areas in East Africa. x and y indicate the contributions of the two members of the pair, but x may sometimes refer to the male and sometimes to the female, and similarly with y. (The figure 8 above the treble clef indicates that all that follows should be read as one octave higher than would otherwise be the case.)(W. H. Thorpe, Phil. Trans. Roy. Soc. B 251, 1966.)

regarded as 'excitement songs', probably having no other function than relieving the bird's pent-up feelings. Such singing is a 'displacement activity' — behaviour performed out of context. Even wounded and dying birds have very occasionally been known to sing — as the Greeks supposed the swan to do.

3. Courtship and nesting song

We have seen that song has a number of functions in the breeding cycle besides being a declaration that an area is under the guardianship of the occupying bird. In relation to females it can be a long-distance invitation, a short-distance stimulant — namely courtship song — or a means whereby the pair-bond is established, maintained and strengthened.

Stimulation

Song is dependent on physiological changes, especially the activity of the gonads and hormone production, which in turn are influenced by environmental factors, particularly increasing daylight in the temperate zones; but psychological stimuli are also important in eliciting song and influencing the female. These may be visual or acoustic, or both. When two pen Mute Swans are in close association egg-laying may occur and ovulation may be induced in a Pigeon placed within sight and hearing of a male. Full ovarian activity occurs in Budgerigars caged in darkness but able to hear males. Isolated Canaries which can hear singing lay earlier than females unable to do so. A female Goldfinch will assume the soliciting posture on hearing, but without seeing, the cock. When a Chaffinch was brought into song by means of injections at an unusual time of year a wild Chaffinch responded by flying close to him and singing.

19. Heron.

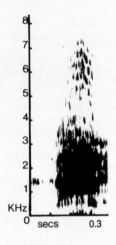

20. The Heron's invitatory call — 'ank'. The call is uttered during a display in which the bird stretches up his neck arched over his back and then brings it down. The movements are somewhat similar to the 'klappering' display of the White Stork and the trumpeting of the King Penguin.

Invitatory song

The three types of song mentioned above cannot always be clearly distinguished because in some species the functions overlap or grade into one another. The Heron's (fig. 19) invitatory display illustrates this as well as the necessity to avoid defining 'song' too rigidly. Early in the year a male secures a stance among the branches of a tall tree and lays a few twigs as a foundation for the nest. Here he stands hour after hour and, if need be, day after day, ever and anon stretching up his neck and arching it over his back so that the decorative plumes are fluffed out. He constantly repeats a sharp barking call, *ank,* or call-song (fig. 20). Sometimes he leans forward and clatters his mandibles — instrumental song — a display with similarities to the White Stork's 'klappering' which, however, is non-vocal. These efforts eventually attract a female but at first he cannot repress his defensive impulses and fends her off. (A similar situation arises when Robins pair up.) She persists, and in course of time an understanding is established and he presents sticks — ceremonially making up to her. Thus his behaviour stimulates her sexually and she becomes his mate.

A ceremony of a similar but simpler character may be seen being enacted on our housetops. A cock House Sparrow monotonously reiterating a chirp from a ledge or gutter is not merely passing the time of day. He is announcing that he has secured a nest-site close by and is pleading for a female to join him.

Among birds which are fine songsters the Blackcap and Garden Warbler invite and stimulate their prospective mates in much the same way, but more melodiously. When a male has laid the foundation of the nest among the twigs of a bush he sings to attract the attention of a female and lure her to it. In those species, such as the Penduline Tit, in which the male builds the nest, he may advertise vocally for a mate while clinging to it (fig. 21).

Such procedures have three aspects or elements: (1) a nesting site is advertised; (2) an invitation is extended to partner the proprietor; and (3) the female is stimulated. Vocalisations as well as movements and posturing all play their part.

In species which rely for nesting on natural cavities the male has to pre-empt suitable accommodation if he is to secure a mate. The Great Tit must find such a site — and in many woods they are in short supply — whereas the Willow Tit hacks out a hole in a rotten tree-stump, also not easy to find except in Arctic forests where the

21. The Penduline Tit's invitatory call uttered while clinging to the nest. The lower part of the sonagram is the song of a Garden Warbler in the background.

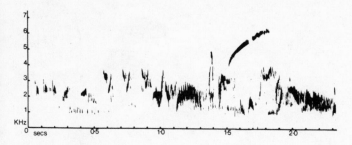

birch trees rot at the level of the deep winter snow. We remedy the deficiency for Great Tits by putting up nesting-boxes. Those who do so may be rewarded by seeing how one of these birds goes about inducing his mate to nest in it. By singing around he attracts her attention and both approach the box. He clings near the entrance and taps vigorously. This tapping might be thought to be token hacking out of a hole, but the Scops Owl taps inside the nest-cavity to attract the female although owls do not excavate cavities. Such tapping can be regarded as a primitive instrumental song. He looks inside and, as he clings, turns his head so that the striking markings are clearly displayed. Then he enters, flies out and sings a modified version of his usual song. He thus indicates the opening and perhaps assures the female that no unpleasant surprise, such as a mouse, awaits her. She approaches timidly, tentatively inspecting the aperture, and enters. If satisfied she soon begins to carry in nest-material. Redstarts and Pied Flycatchers (fig. 22), which appropriate nest-cavities before the females arrive from winter quarters, adopt comparable nest invitation procedures. The cocks may add to the inducements by singing inside the hole.

22. Pied Flycatchers.

Songs on these occasions are usually subdued as is customary with courtship songs and as befits vulnerable conspicuous birds at nest sites.

The American House Wren nests in holes and the cock sings close to the site and from the entrance. He carries in token material while the female he has already attracted looks on. The combined courtship and nest-invitation ceremonial of our Wren is even more pleasant to watch and delightful to listen to. The male constructs several nests and sings vehemently. When a potential mate appears he leads her to one of them, performing his fluttering movements. She acts demurely, creeping about in the herbage and low bushes as if intent on feeding, uttering no sound. You might think she was paying no attention. He dances attendance, springing excitedly from twig to twig with flipping wings, uttering his song in modified forms — often abbreviated but occasionally as a prolonged stream of notes, slower, lower-pitched and more pleasing musically than the territorial song. When the nest is reached the songs become more intense, he darts

23. Crossbills.

inside and flits, singing, to a branch close by. She creeps closer, overcoming her timidity, and at last enters and inspects the proposed domicile (plate 13). She may find it to her liking but, if not, the cock may lead her to another of his nests — for he builds several — where the procedure is repeated. If the nest and its situation please her she settles in, fetching a lining of feathers. He may seek another partner, for where there is good foraging, as in the woods of southern England, Wrens are polygamous, but on the bleak Shetland moors monogamy is the rule as the efforts of both are needed to rear the brood successfully. The nature of the pair-bond in birds is subtly related to conditions in the habitat.

Nest-site selection song

A clear distinction cannot be drawn between invitatory song and nest-site indication song because it is difficult to determine whether in some species the establishment of the pair-bond occurs before, after or during nest-site indication. Birds prospecting for nest-sites may do so together and sometimes give the impression of being in a tense state. The cock Twite may lead the female to a site which he has already found. He sings while she 'makes up her mind'. After a Linnet has drawn attention to a suitable site he emits a subdued, twittering flow of notes. Cock and hen Crossbill (fig. 23) both sing softly as they prospect but even when he places a twig among the pine needles she may not take the hint. Some ground-nesting buntings merely utter a nest-site call similar to the solicitation call.

Song-flight, courtship and nest-indication

Song-flights, whether of only a few feet into the air as by some warblers or of wide scope, such as those of many waders, are performed as courtship and preliminaries to nest-indication. The Greenshank's song-flight involves soaring and circling while making the sky ring with piping *too-hoos* but, more usually, he performs switchback manoeuvres, singing during the gliding descent. When seeking to attract a female a special sex call is introduced and after they have paired up he leads her to one possible site sfter another — usually beside a large boulder. During the Spotted Redshank's song-flight as I have seen it in Lapland, the male flies repeatedly over the marshes to a height of about fifty feet, crying loudly *chup chup chup*, then dives steeply and zig zags close to the ground so that the pale under surface of the wings and white rump contrast strongly with the black underparts. These aerobatics would appear more spectacular to a female beneath the performer than to neighbouring males some distance away so that we may presume them to be sexually stimulatory. The Pectoral Sandpiper, another northern wader, has a striking display — an aerial dance during which resonant

24. *Frigatebirds.*

booming notes are uttered. They are amplified by the inflated air-pouch in the bird's throat. This adaptation adds to the conspicuousness of the performance visually as well as vocally. A number of these birds displaying over the Nearctic tundra look like toy balloons bobbing about. Since this display does not occur when territories are established away from the breeding grounds we may assume that it has courtship significance.

Even more spectacular is the displaying Magnificent Frigatebird equipped with a huge bladder-like scarlet throat sac (fig. 24). Posing on a proposed nest-site the male, clad in iridescent black plumage, rattles his mandibles and wing quills, importuning the females flying overhead. The trees on which these piratical birds perch look as if adorned with bright red blossoms. The throat pouch also serves as a resonance chamber for drumming and clacking noises. Sometimes Frigatebirds, whose wing-span is seven feet, keep their balloons inflated in flight but it is not known whether this aerial display has additional courtship significance. Both sexes of the Mockingthrush — a tropical American species — have inflated sacs on either side of the throat which puff out like yellow cherries when the birds sing.

The cock Yellow Wagtail's close-up display entices and stimulates the female. He sings from a perch close to her, throwing his head back to bring his yellow breast into prominence, then takes off with flickering wings and flutters down nearer to his inamorata singing a simple *sree-sree-sree* — a refined version of his usual call-note. Before copulating he hovers with breast feathers puffed out and tail widely fanned, then alights on the ground and mounts.

Courtship song

We have had to confine our survey to a few instances illustrating the wide range of beautiful courtship and nesting displays in which song occurs. In such displays visual and vocal elements are very closely related. No *prima donna* can surpass a bird in combining gesture, vocal expression and costume to arouse response. Three examples from birds of very different habitats, in Europe, North America and New Guinea will suffice to show that there is a general tendency for courtship song to be subdued and musical.

The courtship of Dippers has similarities to the wooing of Wrens except that, as the pair combine to build the nest, the procedure does not involve leading the female to it and much of the display is mutual. Both quiver their wings and bob up and down while the cock expresses himself in bursts of song. The white breasts are very conspicuous. Like the courting Wren he sustains a sweet subsong. But Dippers differ from Wrens in that the female also sings and joins in the defence of territory — a stretch of stream.

Few brightly coloured birds have loud territorial songs and such species usually have habitat adaptations which reduce their conspicuousness and vulnerability. Rose-breasted Grosbeaks nest where the birds are not easily visible among thick bushes and tall, succulent vegetation. The courting male crouches before the hen, moving his head back and forth while pouring out a soft, continuous melodious song — some notes of which are inaudible more than a few feet away. This whisper song is very different from the territorial song. As he sings he dances erratically like a splendid butterfly, displaying the blacks and whites of the underwing coverts and white rump. Coition follows, and then he flies to a branch and sings loudly the territorial song. Such post-coital song occurs in a number of species.

The courtship song-and-dance of the King Bird of Paradise is particularly splendid. The male begins by uttering various calls, then opens and flaps his wings, making a half-turn to face the female, puffing out his silky white feathers and warbling in a manner reminiscent of a distant Skylark. He opens and shuts his side plumes and throws forward over his head the long and slender tail quills which are so feathered at the tips as to look like burnished green discs as they are tossed from side to side. His swaying body keeps time with the song. He concludes with an

25. Penduline Tit.

about-turn, bends down, opens his mouth widely so that the green inner coloration is displayed and sings a few final gurgling notes.

Pre-coitional and coitional songs and calls
    The females of many species utter solicitation calls if the male shows insufficient ardour. Most bird-watchers will have noticed the wing-quivering and squealing of the hen House Sparrow craving the cock's attention. The Hawfinch accompanies her wing-fluttering with a wheezing *zee-zee*. Male birds may call or sing before, during or after copulation. The Swallow and Sand Martin sing as a prelude to the act, the Woodlark and Hedgesparrow sing during it, and after it the Greenfinch sings briefly and the Scarlet

Grosbeak twitters subsong. The Domestic Cock crows after treading the hen.

Nest-building song

Song by a bird engaged in building is unusual, partly because nest-construction is commonly the responsibility of the songless female, partly because the attention of predators might thus be drawn to the nest and, also, to some extent, because energy and attention devoted to one form of behaviour reduce that available for another. As we have noted the cock Penduline Tit (fig. 25) sings as he builds (fig. 21). Some weaverbirds utter advertising songs or calls near to or clinging near to the nest. Like the Penduline Tit and Oropendola they construct pendant nests, safe from all but flying predators. The Wren may sing snatches near the nest in intervals between building and when he makes routine visits of inspection. In all these species the male's songs or calls are important in attracting the female and drawing her attention to the domicile he has prepared. In such circumstances it pays to advertise if the contents of the nest are not endangered. Jacamars call while excavating their burrows in steep banks, Sand Martins call around their colonies in similar situations out of reach of predators and the cock Nuthatch, singing close to where his mate is building, is unlikely to jeopardise the eggs, soon to be laid in the hole in a vertical tree-trunk with the entrance narrowed and fortified with a plastering of mud. In Britain the land-bird noisiest at the nest is the Rook. Its nests are difficult to reach and few four-footed marauders would risk a combined assault by an angry gang while out on a limb. Herons are also clamorous but they, too, usually nest in high trees though I was once able to step into a deserted nest and sit down there. It was on a low bush growing on a small marine island and had been robbed by creatures more mischievous than breeding Herons had previously encountered — boys.

Incubation song

Obviously any bird which sang loudly while sitting on eggs would be courting disaster so incubation song, which is uncommon, is subdued and uttered by birds in relatively safe nesting-sites. Rooks, Carrion Crows and Jays twitter their very quiet, crackling songs without any risk of betraying the whereabouts of the nest. This kind of song, comparable with a cat's purring, seems to indicate contentment. The Jackdaw has an incubation song like the Carrion Crow's but also sings a quiet, rippling subsong incorporating calls and mimicries. (A number of birds sing subsong of this kind before they come into full song.) Sitting female Blackcaps and Rose-breasted Grosbeaks sing softly but a Reed Warbler occasionally sings loudly from his hammock in the reeds. The nests of this species, surrounded by water and upheld by slippery reeds, are not easily plundered although Cuckoos manage to lay in them. They find them beforehand by watching the birds but corvine predators seem to rely more on systematic searching for nests than on noticing birds building.

Nest-relief song

In some species the brooding bird calls or sings to indicate that it is time for his or her partner to take over, or the male may call his mate off. Among American species, a Black-headed Grosbeak answers her mate with a song similar to his when he comes to relieve her, Rose-breasted Grosbeaks sing quietly and Brown Thrashers utter a subdued song as a hint to the cock to take over. Normally Hawfinches are secretive near the nest but the male gives a quiet *quilp* to call his mate off. When he feeds her on the nest he chatters softly. In some species the cock comes to the nest after a due interval and his mate joins him when he sings or calls. Thus territorial song may be used specifically to call a bird's mate.

Male and female Great Northern Divers take turns on the eggs and the sitting bird gives a loud wail repeatedly when wanting to be relieved. When I surprised one near the nest it reared up erect, standing on the water uttering a startling yell. Gannets participate in an elaborate nest-relief ceremony, clashing bills and calling hoarsely. Shearwaters cackle, crow and croon together in their burrows. Fulmars squat on the nest-site opening their beaks widely as they utter guttural calls (plate 9). Mutual ceremonies are usual among similarly plumaged sea-birds. Such rituals occur in other groups. The cock Nightjar flies close to where his well-camouflaged mate is brooding amidst the bracken. He gives a call not heard at any other time and she replies with subdued churring. Borne on silent wings he alights on the ground by her side and they squat together, churring and swaying. Suddenly the female flies off, leaving him to brood.

4. Communication between parents and young

The arrival of their first baby involves new orientations for husband and wife — a delightful, stimulating situation but involving anticipatory preparations and some anxieties. Among birds comparable tensions and changes of routine occur; but the emergence of a living creature from a hard object which has been incubated for days or weeks does not come without intimations of what is about to happen.

Communication before and after hatching

Birds as different as the Redstart and Chough may bring food before the eggs have hatched. A female Chough was seen to regurgitate into the nest and utter the feeding call nearly two hours before the first egg was pipped and more than eight hours before it hatched. Perhaps such feeding or false-feeding activities may sometimes appear prematurely because of physiological changes in the brooding bird but certainly sounds from within the egg often give warning.

As Guillemots lay a single, large, pyriform egg on a rock ledge it is easy for an observer to see what happens during the critical period. Four and a half days before the hatch scraping noises and faint squeaking may be heard. The pair show their interest and agitation by leaning over the egg, flapping their wings, fidgeting with scraps, uttering the feeding call and bringing fish. The hatch may take three and a half days and during this period rapport is established between parents and chick. While still in the egg it is able to distinguish the significance of certain calls. To some extent it recognises its parents acoustically before it is able to do so visually.

Embryonic signals and tactile sounds

It has long been known that the tapping of the chick's beak, furnished with the 'egg-tooth', indicates that the youngster is about to emerge. The brooding parent is thus made aware of what is happening. Vocal calls may also be heard from unhatched eggs and two-way communication established (fig. 26). Mallard ducklings respond to parental calls some days before they hatch. Apart from these tactile and vocal sounds clicks are audible when the egg of a duck, hen or gull is held to the ear. These are caused by respiratory movements but other noises within the egg are due

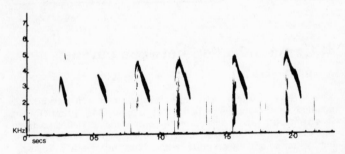

26. The tapping and calls of a Partridge chick at least 24 hours before hatching.

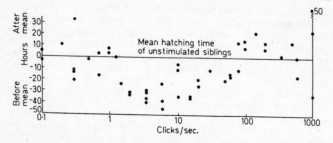

27. The hatching times of isolated Japanese Quail chicks compared with that of chicks in the clutch, showing that sounds from within the egg tend to synchronise hatching. (M. A. Vince, Brit. Poult. Sci. 9, 1968.)

to the embryo changing position. Such various sounds are effective as communication from egg to egg for it has been shown that they bring about a synchronous hatch (fig. 27). In some species this can be of vital importance because the survival of ducklings and other young birds which can run soon after hatching depends on being able to follow the parent as a family. In other species, especially owls, whose food supply is uncertain, the reverse applies and 'spread' in hatching may be advantageous.

Song while tending young

A Blackbird, Blackcap or Whitethroat feeding young may sing snatches as he comes or goes. In Lapland I watched a Redwing sing now and then as the young left the nest at midnight. The cock Nightingale takes responsibility for feeding the young on the day they hatch. One was seen to approach the nest in a state of great excitement and, holding a beakful of grubs, perch above where his mate was covering the chicks and pour out a stream of bubbling notes so subdued as to be inaudible more than a few feet away (plate 15).

The extent to which territorial song continues after the young hatch varies so much from species to species and according to circumstances that generalisations are precarious. It depends on such factors as the nature of the pair-bond, the number of broods, and the assiduity of the cock in feeding the chicks. A cock Chaffinch increases his singing when the chicks are about to fledge. The Wren, being polygamous, continues actively in song after installing a mate in one of his nests. Of course, when a male is strenuously feeding the brood his songfulness decreases or ceases. The relationship between songfulness and the breeding cycle in birds deserves further study. In some species it is highly important that chicks should hear their father's song for thus the young of such birds as the Bullfinch and Zebra Finch learn to sing it.

Females may sing when tending or brooding the nestlings, usually very quietly. I have known a female Wren sing a chittering whisper song over the newly hatched chicks so softly that I was only able to hear it with my ear a few inches away. Perhaps this whispering encourages the young to beg but some newly hatched nestlings seem to respond very little to sounds. Later, although hungry chicks make their demands evident vocally, parents may use calls to stimulate them to open their bills. The arrival of the parent is usually the signal to beg.

Some woodpeckers twitter as they brood the nestlings. This kind of subdued, simple song has been noted of few open-nesting birds, except, as we have seen, during incubation, but a female Greenfinch may warble as she stands over the young.

Begging calls

In many passerine species the nestling begs on its first day and the calls of the brood become louder as they grow. A compromise achieved through natural selection ensures that nestlings plead loud enough to encourage their parents to feed them but not so vigorously or frequently as to betray them to predators. There is a relationship between the degree of protection provided by the situation of the nest and the volume and persistence of begging. Young Kingfishers, safe in a burrow in a vertical bank rising from a stream, make a continuous trilling noise and woodpecker chicks emit sizzling or 'scissoring' sounds. In contrast to the noisiness of young Rooks, nestling Carrion Crows are quiet. Crows, unlike Rooks, have no neighbouring kin to respond to alarm cries and join in mobbing intruders.

Communication when the young leave the nest

The begging call of nestling passerines commonly changes to a combined hunger and contact call when they leave the nest, or just before. Nestlings usually depart spontaneously when they are sufficiently mature but the parents, especially in species with covered nests, may attract them out. A female Wren sometimes uses her twittering whisper song to lead forth the young and woodpeckers may lure out the young by calling. Young Great Tits emerge of their own accord but as soon as the male notices what is happening he gives a *see-saw* song or call of about seven notes which is used on other occasions to attract the brood. The

Goldfinch uses a musical trisyllabic call to attract the fledged young to be fed. A cock Partridge was seen to dance here and there excitedly when he first caught sight of the newly-hatched young. Contact notes enable families to keep together. This is specially important in ground-nesting species with chicks able to run soon after hatching. If a chick is unable to answer the mother may kill it.

Alarm calls

On hearing the parent's alarm notes the young of most species react to them as warnings and become silent and still, whether in the nest or outside it. Oystercatchers and Ringed Plovers fly around frantically sounding the alarm when a predator approaches and immediately the chicks crouch immobile. They are so camouflaged that they are difficult to detect on the ground or shingle. Once in the Alps I nearly stepped on what I took to be a rounded boulder on the steep path and was startled when it exploded into flight uttering a harsh alarm call. The ground where the Ptarmigan had been squatting low over her chicks came to life as they scurried to cover in all directions. So nimble and protectively coloured were they that I was able to find only two of a family of about eight.

Attack and distraction display calls

When a bird is disturbed at the nest it may fly right away, as a Golden Eagle does if the intruder is a man, or move around sounding alarm or distress calls. The Eider Duck may remain and even allow herself to be stroked. In contrast some birds make more or less serious attacks, even on human beings. A Great Skua swoops aggressively uttering a harsh cry and sometimes knocking off one's hat. A Brown Owl may press home a damaging onslaught. The Snowy Owl's display is a compromise between attacking and fleeing (fig. 6). It will hunch up, giving threat calls, and then flop away with drooping wings. In conflict situations birds sometimes make confused responses, hesitating between two contrary activities, and these may become ritualised — that is become such that they are elicited instinctively and acquire signal significance. Thus a Kittiwake when confronted by another turns away its head (plate 8); a wolf in a similar situation will do likewise. This has become an appeasing gesture — 'I don't want to fight'.

Some birds behave in a way which we may regard as an elaborated version of the Snowy Owl's display — a ritualised conflict response which has great survival value for ground-nesting species. They sprawl on the ground as if injured, wings extended, seemingly useless, sometimes squealing or squeaking in a way which calls attention to what they are doing. The Ringed

Plover, Dotterel and American Killdeer Plover are noted for the realism of their 'distraction displays'. So strong was the conflict between a Ringed Plover's urge to remain brooding the eggs that I was able to put my hand under her breast but if I alarmed her slightly she scuttled away 'injury-feigning'. I could do this again and again because she always quickly returned to incubate. Occasionally a bird in such a conflict situation acts incongruously. A cock Lapwing accompanied his distraction display with sexual calls when a sheep approached the nest where the eggs were chipping and when a Blue Tit's chick gave a cry of pain a parent flew near it hissing continuously and holding up a wing for two or three seconds. Investigation of such confused responses should lead to a deeper understanding of the springs of behaviour.

Roosting calls and songs

When Great Tits are at the nest-building stage the male accompanies his mate to the cavity and continues to inspect it after she has entered to spend the night, uttering call-notes and sometimes singing. He goes to roost elsewhere but arrives back before sunrise and sings varied songs. When she emerges he immediately tries to copulate. Great Tits do not lead the fledged young back to the nest-cavity to roost but after young Wrens leave the nest for the first time the male sings around and at dusk may attract them to sleeping quarters in one of his other nests or the disused nest of some other bird — sometimes an open nest. Usually, when the family is safely ensconced he goes to roost elsewhere. The female may guide the party, flying ahead by fits and starts; and when the roost is reached she may sing 'whisper song' as she puts the family to bed. This procedure of leading the young to roost is a reminder that the Wren's remote ancestors came from the American tropics where a number of Wren species escort the fledged young to auxiliary nests. Some construct nests to serve as dormitories. Probably this adaptation, involving taking refuge at night in nests, originated as a means of escaping attack from the predatory birds and beasts which are active nocturnally in tropical forests, but when the Wren travelled to Asia and so to Europe by way of Bering Strait and established itself in colder regions communal roosting had the additional advantage of enabling these small birds to conserve heat. Not only the young are led to roost. At dusk on cold winter nights you may glimpse a little party, led by a singing bird, making for shelter in a disused nest, sometimes a House Martin's.

Most European birds have simpler procedures. Whitethroats utter *tick* notes and also soft, grating calls as the birds move along a hedgerow in a loose group. The parents bring food from time to time but as darkness falls the fledglings are left to themselves, huddled two or three together about a man's height from the ground. The Ringed Plover calls her chicks together on an open bank of shingle and broods over them throughout the night.

5. How birds acquire their songs

As we all know, parrots can be taught to 'talk' to the extent of learning to say a number of words or short sentences if they hear them frequently. In contrast, a Cuckoo, reared in the nest of a Hedgesparrow or Reed Warbler and never hearing the double note, is able to sing it correctly when he returns after wintering in Africa. Thus in different species the capacity to learn sounds varies immensely. There are such differences between species that it is unwise to generalise but it may be said that the birds not usually classed as song-birds normally have the inborn capacity to utter their whole repertoire whereas song-birds commonly have some learning ability, so far as song is concerned, though their calls are usually innate. The extent to which a bird has to learn its song from others can only be ascertained by studying how it develops in individuals.

Song development: Whitethroat

A few examples of how song is acquired follow. The Whitethroat has a repertoire of twenty-five call-notes and three kinds of song. As with many other species the calls are innate; and so, to a considerable extent, are the songs. Song matures, beginning with a single note comparable with the nestling's begging call. (Nestling and fledgling calls generally disappear on independence being attained but they may contribute to other vocalisations or recur during courtship.) As the days pass additional notes are heard until the young male is uttering a subdued, rambling song. Like most such developmental subsong it is uttered from cover and is not territorial. A certain amount of song is heard from Whitethroats in their African winter quarters and on spring passage in Italy. Males arriving back in spring may still sing this inward, juvenile type of subsong but when aroused by the challenge of a rival male or the approach of a female they break out into full territorial song. This is of two kinds, gentle and vigorous, depending on the degree of stimulation. When a female lingers in or near the territory the full song is heard in display flight, the bird mounting up a short distance from a bush, jingling out his little ditty. This combined song and dance attracts and stimulates her. As is customary with many species song decreases as nesting proceeds but it persists from mid April to July. Females recognise that a male not singing is already mated or otherwise unsuitable as a partner and go elsewhere.

Chaffinch

In autumn young Chaffinches develop a subsong which at first is only a quiet series of chirping notes, fluctuating in pitch. Later, rattling sounds are introduced. By the end of March in the first breeding season the song is Chaffinch-like but loosely constructed. In May and June it becomes integrated and normal (fig. 28). If, however, a young bird is brought up in isolation he sings normal subsong but in default of hearing other Chaffinches his song becomes and remains abnormal. Its length, number of notes, and to some extent tonality, are approximately correct but other characteristics are missing. This kind of experiment shows that elements of the song, a kind of imperfect blueprint, are inborn.

In the wild the young Chaffinch learns some characteristics of his song from the male parent or other males during the first month or two of life at a period when there is a good deal of song, but not until the following spring does he acquire the finer details by hearing neighbouring birds. Although a Chaffinch might seem to sing the same phrase all the time, sonagrams show that this is not so. Each individual has a repertoire of up to six song-types. (Some other species have considerably more.) As Chaffinches compete they learn song-types from one other. This learning of song-types tends to maintain 'dialects' in some areas. Each song-type is typically Chaffinch-like but has its own peculiarities. An individual sings one song-type for a spell, then changes to another — thus avoiding excessive monotony. When singing against a neighbour a mature Chaffinch tends to use the song-type in his repertoire most like his — throwing it back at him as if to say, 'This is meant for you'. The learning ability of the Chaffinch ceases when he is about thirteen months old.

Blackbird

Blackbird song is of the continuous type in contrast with the phrase type of the Chaffinch and buntings in which there are definite intervals between the separate utterances. Newly fledged young emit a subdued *reereeree* but about the nineteenth day the juvenile song begins to be heard — a quiet, rambling series of notes. At first the duration of the song is brief but after a few days it may be sustained for as long as half an hour. As in the Skylark's territorial song alarm notes may be interspersed. This is also typical of the subsong when an adult Blackbird is coming into song in Spring. The song of a young Blackbird brought up in isolation approximates to the normal song but is deficient in some respects. Blackbirds learn from neighbours, particularly between Christmas and March when subsong is often heard during mild weather. They utter phrases acquired the previous year and, as time goes on, the song becomes loud and typical. Individuals vary in their ability to elaborate their songs. A bird may begin the

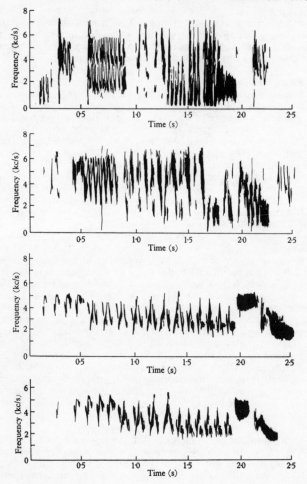

28. The development of Chaffinch song: (top) subsong, showing chirps and rattles with a great range of frequencies; (second from top) subsong in transition to full song; (third from top) song of young bird on 4th May; (bottom) song of the same bird four days later showing the rapidity of the process of tightening and integration. (W. H. Thorpe, 'Bird-song', C.U.P., 1961.)

season with forty motifs and by redistribution and combination create as many as ninety phrases. The process involves adding, altering, selecting and improvising (fig. 16). According to our standards some songs become more musical as the season advances and their territorial importance wanes.

Copying sounds

Birds may learn songs before they are able to sing — as a book may be set in type months before it is printed and published. A Nightingale at the age of six weeks heard a Blackcap for ten days; when he came into song the following year he sang this song perfectly. Normally young Nightingales learn some details of their father's song soon after leaving the nest but they do not reproduce them until seven months later (plate 15). A Bullfinch, too, learns the male parent's song, as already mentioned, but this is not merely due to his singing close at hand but to the intimate relationship between young and old. When a Bullfinch is reared with Canaries he learns his foster-father's song even if he is able to hear other Bullfinches.

Mimicry

It is customary to speak of mimicry when the vocalisations learned and reproduced are not those of the species, such as the song-types which the Chaffinch acquires, but of another species or some extraneous sound as when a Marsh Warbler or Blackcap copies other birds (fig. 29). From ancient times it has been known that some birds can learn to repeat words. Although many wild birds copy the vocalisations of other species, especially in subsong, neither the Indian Hill Myna nor parrots, both noted for their imitativeness, have been heard to mimic alien sounds in their native haunts. Mimicry does not develop unless these birds are prevented from mixing naturally with others of their kind. Deprived of normal social opportunities they become attentive and receptive to a wide range of sounds. Apparently when a bird learns a few words from his owner he is reaching out for the fellowship with his own kind unattainable in captivity.

Exceptions are so numerous that scarcely any generalisation concerning mimicry is valid. Few birds learn mimicries after they are two years old but parrots older than this may still acquire them. Some, such as the Chaffinch, can only learn songs with some similarity to their own — such as the Tree Pipit's — whereas the Lyrebird can imitate the hooting of cars and the Spotted Bowerbird is said to reproduce the barking of dogs and twanging of wire fences. Some fifty Australian and thirty British species are, to some extent, mimics.

Emotional attachment or individual rapport is favourable to learning alien sounds but mimicries may also be acquired by birds

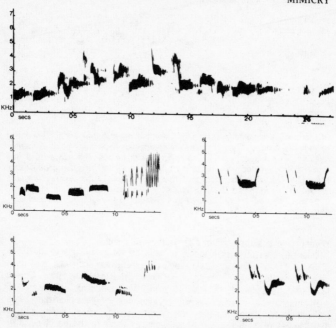

29. Sonagrams: (top) normal Blackcap song; (left centre) Blackbird song; (right centre) Song Thrush song; (left bottom) imitation of Blackbird by Blackcap; (right bottom) imitation of Song Thrush by Blackcap. The Song Thrush expression sounds like 'Mrs Hewitt, Mrs Hewitt'.

in a state of alarm or excitement. 'Talking' birds may even learn the appropriate occasions on which to make remarks. My wife had a parrot at her home in Brazil which greeted the butcher, but never the milkman, with 'Is the meat tender today?' An Amazon Parrot may acquire a vocabulary of between fifty and a hundred words.

Occasionally birds are accidentally alarmed by the fortuitous imitation of one of their warning calls by another species. A flock of Smooth-billed Anis flew up when a Mockingbird uttered their alarm cry and a hen and her chicks made for cover when a Spotted Bowerbird imitated a Whistling Eagle.

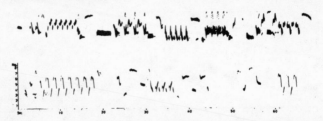

30. A comparison of Wren songs illustrating subspecific differences: (above) Hebrides, 'Troglodytes t. hebridensis', (below) Sark, Channel Islands, 'T. t. troglodytes'. The songs are of almost the same duration and there are repetitive sections in both, three in the utterance of the type species and five in that of the Hebridean Wren. In this respect the latter is closer to the North American subspecies 'T. t. hiemalis' but scrutiny of more recordings would be required before any conclusions could be drawn.

Dialects and subspecific differences in song

If a population of a species is isolated long enough it tends to diverge from the original stock in song as well as physical characteristics. The Wrens of continental Europe, Outer Hebrides, Shetland, St Kilda and Iceland are all separate subspecies of *Troglodytes troglodytes*. Their songs are immediately recognisable as Wren songs but with slight differences more apparent in sonagrams than to the ear (fig. 30). So, too, with the subspecies *hiemalis* as I heard it on the summit of the Smoky Mountains in North Carolina. Thousands of years have elapsed since Wrens crossed Bering Strait and Asia to settle in Europe's western isles and yet the song has undergone comparatively little change — due to genetic changes more than to learning.

Dialect changes are primarily due to learning — one bird imitating another throughout a population. This has been shown to be true of the American White-crowned Sparrow. The extension of a dialect variation over a period of more than fifty years has been observed. It was first noticed among Blackcaps in the Alps and has now extended through southern Germany, southern France and Spain, spreading at the rate of about five kilometres a year.

The extent to which song changes influence differentiation into species is debatable. In Spain, where there are no breeding Willow Warblers, the Chiffchaff has a very uncharacteristic song but this does not prevent interbreeding where Chiffchaff populations singing the two kinds of song overlap around the Pyrenees. On the other hand when an Indian Great Tit — a different subspecies —

was released in an English wood the resident Great Tits did not recognise nor respond to his calls. If two populations differing in call-notes to this extent — and perhaps also in habitat preferences — were to come into contact these differences might be sufficient to prevent interbreeding and encourage divergence resulting eventually in a new species.

There are great similarities in appearance between the Treecreeper and the Short-toed Treecreeper where the two species overlap on the Continent but the vocalisations and habitat preferences differ, though either species may occasionally learn to sing the song of the other (plate 7). Evidently the original population was divided into two when the ice came south some thousands of years ago. The developments which took place in song, habitat preference, roosting behaviour and foraging habits were sufficient to keep the two populations separate as different species when the populations met and overlapped.

6. Song and the environment

It will already have been evident that if we are to appreciate a bird's songs and calls and understand why they are as they are we must take into consideration its whole mode of life. They must be viewed as subtly integrated into a whole pattern of adaptations. Here only very brief consideration can be given to some of the ways in which vocalisations are related to habitat and co-ordinated with other forms of behaviour.

Internal changes and seasonal activities

Birds concentrate their reproductive activities into a period or periods of the year when conditions are most suitable. The activity of the gonads brings about great changes in physiology and consequently in behaviour. These include seeking out a territory and breeding site — which for some species may involve a journey of thousands of miles — singing or calling, displaying and nest-building. Correlation between the internal physiological situation and external conditions is essential to success. If the environmental situation is unfavourable, as when drought prevails, birds may not even attempt to breed.

Light

Outside tropical regions the most important external factor in bringing about the growth and activity of the gonads together with the production of reproductive cells and hormones is increasing day-length. Songfulness and reproductive activity are associated, though in some species song, with defence of territory, persists beyond the breeding season. Competition and environmental stringencies necessitate compromises in reproductive adaptations; for example, in high latitudes birds gain longer daylight in which to forage for their young but food may be scarcer and the breeding season shorter. The Song Thrush can rear three or even four broods in Italy but only one in southern Finland; but the clutches there are larger.

The 'bird clock'

In the temperate zone the increasing light of the rising sun gives each species its cue to emerge and join the bird chorus. The springtime sequence in an English wood is something like this: Blackbird, Song Thrush, Woodpigeon, Robin, Mistle Thrush, Turtle Dove, Pheasant, Willow Warbler, Wren, Great Tit, House Sparrow, Blue Tit, Chaffinch, Whitethroat. Of these the first would be heard, on average, about forty-four minutes before sunrise and the latest some six minutes before. In spring birds tend to be active earlier relative to light than in winter. At night they tend to go to roost in the reverse sequence to that in which they rise, early risers retiring, and singing, late.

Weather

By reducing light, clouds delay the onset of song and speed birds to roost in the evening. In foggy weather there is less Skylark song and the birds do not fly so high. Strong winds reduce song in some species but have less effect on those which frequent dense cover.

Temperature

The relationship between temperature and song is difficult to assess exactly. Apart from other considerations the inhibiting effect of adverse temperature tends to be less when a bird's ardour is greatest. In spring, when the Chaffinch comes into song a cold spell tends to silence him but the Great Tit's singing is less affected by temperature changes. Pied Flycatchers are among the species which sing more readily in relatively high temperatures. Extremes, high or low, reduce song but species vary greatly in their adaptations to temperature. It may have a powerful indirect effect by influencing the availability of food animals and consequently on vigour and behaviour.

Relationships between adaptations

Only in special circumstances — and these involve various habitat adaptations — can birds afford to make themselves conspicuous vocally as well as visually because double conspicuousness makes things too easy for predators. Each species reaches its own compromise. When we set out the adaptations which accompany the two extremes we are in a better position to decide why a bird sings or calls as it does. But in Europe we need to remind ourselves that man has changed much of the continent and, indeed, of the world, so greatly that extensive habitats with organisms in completely natural relationships to one another are hard to find.

Adaptations correlated respectively with vocal and visual conspicuousness

	VOCAL	VISUAL
Structural	Small size and weak armament	Large size and strong armament
Plumage	Inconspicuous	Conspicuous
Habitat	Dense	Open
Territorialism	Strong	Weak
Pair-bond	Short	Prolonged
Nesting	Isolated	Social
Foraging	Fixed area around nest	Extensive
Predation	Vulnerable	Less vulnerable

It would require more space than is available here to analyse the significance of these contrasts and to consider the factors which account for exceptions but we may compare two species representative of the two categories, vocal and visual — the Nightingale and the Herring Gull. The comparison is crude as normally other factors have to be taken into consideration but it serves to illustrate the principles involved. The former is a small brown migratory passerine with a beak adapted for picking up small organisms and unsuited for defence. It nests in deciduous woods, spinneys, thickets and hedgerows and the foraging area is mainly the territory which the male defends with song. Being subject to the hazards of migration the pair-bond lasts no longer than is necessary to rear a single brood. The bird and its brown eggs are inconspicuous. In contrast, the Herring Gull utters loud, unmusical calls and is large, bold and powerful. Its conspicuousness does not endanger it except when it chooses an abnormally accessible nesting site. Indeed, its predominantly white coloration is advantageous, enabling a number of birds to exploit a temporary food supply. It breeds socially, gaining additional protection from predators thereby, and defends from its fellows only the area immediately around the nest. It is monogamous and mates for life, the pairs meeting again at the breeding grounds each spring, recognising each other by voice as well as appearance. Herring gulls feed far and wide on marine organisms, carrion and what they can scavenge, sometimes inland.

Diet

Investigation of the feeding behaviour of any of the larger organisms, whether the birds in our woods or the mammals on an East African plain, shows that in general, although there can be overlapping in food choices, no species is in direct competition with any other occupying the same habitat. Although several species of tit may live together in a wood they feed at different levels in the foliage and each selects its prey according to its particular adaptations — although when there is a caterpillar 'plague' all may rally to the feast.

There are subtle relationships between what a bird eats, its other adaptations and its vocalisations but we must confine ourselves to a few broad generalisations. The list given above suggests that there is truth in the saying 'the early bird gets the worm', for of the five earliest risers all but the Woodpigeon feed to some extent on earthworms, snails and slugs which are most available before warmth and light cause them to withdraw. The Woodpigeon and Turtle Dove being grazers and taking a very wide range of vegetable food, are able to feed early. Insectivorous and grain-eating birds come next in order but some insect-eaters, such as the large-eyed Robin able to discern prey in poor light, tend to rise, feed and sing before graminivorous species. Some seed-eaters are good songsters but those which are also gregarious mostly have rather subdued, twittering songs. They can afford to be gregarious, even in their nesting behaviour, as their food, weed seeds and grain, is often abundant enough to satisfy all. This also applies to some berry- and fruit-eating birds, including the waxwings and a number of tropical species, few of which are notable songsters. However, some good singers, such as Larks, eat seeds as well as insects.

Aerial insect-feeders — swallows, swifts, martins and bee-eaters — also nest colonially and are mediocre singers. Carrion-feeding species do not sing. The vultures croak and hiss and the Raven and crows call loudly. Like such fish-eaters as the Gannet and tropicbirds they gather where food becomes plentiful and rely to some extent on visual signals — the movements of other birds in the air — to locate carcasses. Summing up, excellence in song is correlated with territorialism, invertebrate diet, sober plumage, and, with qualifications, concealing habitat.

Vegetation

There is a tendency for species living in low homogeneous vegetation to utter repetitive calls or songs. Two birds of grassland, the Corncrake, which reiterates its Latin name *Crex crex*, and the Quail, with his *'wet my lips'*, are often heard by night — when the females fly in — as well as by day. As they are doubly concealed by darkness and vegetation and their sojourn in the north is brief it is of prime importance that the males should advertise where they are loudly and persistently in order to obtain mates promptly.

A number of passerine song-birds which frequent reed-beds have continuous-type songs, either high-pitched, sibilant and reiterative or garrulous, varied and, to some extent, imitative. The songs of the Grasshopper and Savi's Warblers are of the first types. Among singers of the second type are the Reed, Great Reed, Sedge (plate 1) and Marsh Warblers. Both types have carrying power above the whispering of the wind in the reeds. All these species sing to a minor extent nocturnally. Contact notes have special importance for Bearded Tits which move about the reed-beds in parties. Their clinking calls are unlike any other sounds in their habitat.

Another type of highly reiterative, far-carrying, distinctive song is the drumming of woodpeckers, audible for a long distance above the noises of wind in the foliage. It may be significant that of the three British woodpeckers the Green, which seldom drums, is the species which spends most time outside woodland.

Loud song, uttered by many species on the wing and thus adding to its range and the singer's conspicuousness is characteristic of birds of open spaces — prairie, tundra, moorland and desert. The vehement calling of marine species is a concomitant of their gregarious nesting.

Of course there are exceptions to these generalisations concerning the adaptations of birds' utterances to their environments, as is to be expected when one factor out of a whole pattern is considered in isolation as responsible for types of song. There is no more fascinating topic to which those who would discover more about bird song could turn their attention than the harmonious inter-relationships between behavioural and ecological adaptations.

7. The study of bird song

The amateur lacks the resources of the professional ornithologist and is handicapped by having to treat the study of bird song as a spare-time occupation but he should make the most of his advantages. He can concentrate on a particular species, common and convenient to study because readily observable near where he lives, or on a less common bird within reasonable distance. There is much still to be learned concerning the songs and calls of even those species on which monographs have been written. Bird-listeners resident for years in any area are able to make long-term observations. Nobody who has studied a species for less than several years can claim to know it. Moreover, intensive observations in one area may reveal adaptations differing from those in other areas such as dialect and breeding-cycle variations. The ecological and behavioural aspects of bird vocalisations are well worth exploring, especially as elaborate apparatus is not required. Further research is needed concerning the influence of environmental factors on bird song — habitat, weather, the pair-bond, and so forth. Each of us should enjoy birds in his or her own way but keeping notes of the relationship between a bird's utterances and its other activities adds interest and value to our observations.

Like bird photography, recording song can be regarded as a separate hobby or an aid to scientific study. Topics worth investigating with a tape-recorder are: the development of song from the nestling stage onwards, mimicry, and subsong. Good results can be obtained with a portable tape-recorder, and by using a parabolic reflector a singing bird can be brought into sharp acoustic focus without intrusive background noises. The diameter of the parabola must be greater than the wave length of the sounds to be recorded. Obviously the bulkier the apparatus the more difficult it is to carry it off the beaten track and mobilise it when an opportunity unexpectedly occurs to record some exceptional utterance. Having secured an imperfect recording a better result may sometimes be obtained by playing it over and so luring the bird to treat the loudspeaker as a rival and sing close to the microphone. This technique should be used with discretion. Photographs of birds in song can be obtained thus. A number of the illustrations reproduced here were taken in this way.

The bulletin *Biophon*, published from the Natural History Museum, University of Aarhus, Denmark, and edited by the International Bio-acoustics Council, lists recordings and comments on technical advances. A *Catalogue of Natural History Recordings* (with supplement) is published by the BBC and mention of discs and other recordings of birds appears in *Discovering Bird Watching* by Jim Flegg in this series. From time to time reviews of recordings appear in *The Ibis* and other ornithological journals. The Cornell Laboratory of Ornithology, 159 Sapsucker Woods Road, Ithaca, New York 14850, has specialised in bird recording and houses an extensive library of tapes and discs from many parts of the world. Another extensive collection of recordings is kept by the British Library of Wildlife Sounds, 29 Exhibition Road, London SW7.

Bibliography

Armstrong, E. A.; *A Study of Bird Song;* Dover, New York, 1973.
Armstrong, E. A.; *Bird Display and Behaviour;* Dover, New York, 1965.
Hartshorne, C.; *Born to Sing;* Indiana University Press, 1973.
Hinde, R. (ed.); *Bird Vocalizations;* Cambridge University Press, 1969.
Jellis, R. E.;*Bird Sounds and their Meanings;* BBC, London, 1977.
Thorpe, W. H.; *Bird-Song;* Cambridge University Press, 1961.

These books provide references to most of the literature on bird song. Some of the *New Naturalist Monographs* (Collins) discuss the vocalisations of particular species.

Index

Printed by C. I. Thomas & Sons (Haverfordwest) Ltd., Press Buildings,
Merlin's Bridge, Haverfordwest, Pembrokeshire.